SLAVERY *and the* COMING *of the* CIVIL WAR

1831–1861

SLAVERY *and the* COMING *of the* CIVIL WAR

1831–1861

Christopher Collier
James Lincoln Collier

BENCHMARK BOOKS

MARSHALL CAVENDISH
NEW YORK

ACKNOWLEDGMENT: The authors wish to thank Stanley L. Engerman, Professor of Economics and History, University of Rochester, for his careful reading of the text of this volume of The Drama of American History and his thoughtful and useful comments. The work has been much improved by his notes. The authors are deeply in his debt, but of course, assume full responsibility for the substance of the work, including any errors.

Photo research by James Lincoln Collier.
COVER PHOTO: © Joslyn Art Museum
PICTURE CREDITS: The photographs in this book are used by permission and through the courtesy of :
Jamestown/Yorktown Fondation: 11(top). Corbis-Bettmann: 13, 14, 17, 22, 25, 27, 28, 32, 36, 39 (top), 39 (bottom), 42, 44, 48, 49, 51 (top), 51 (bottom), 54, 57, 58, 59, 60, 61, 64 (top), 64 (bottom), 67, 68, 69, 71 (top), 71 (bottom), 73, 75. Library of Congress: 18, 40, 43, 78.

Benchmark Books
Marshall Cavendish Corporation
99 White Plains Road
Tarrytown, New York 10591-9001

©2000 Christopher Collier and James Lincoln Collier

Library of Congress Cataloging-in-Publication Data

Collier, Christopher, date
Slavery and the Coming of the Civil War, 1831-1861 / Christopher Collier, James Lincoln Collier.
p.   cm.   —   (The drama of American history)
Includes bibliographical references and index.
Summary: Discusses attitudes and events that led up to the Civil War,
particularly the institution of slavery.
ISBN 0-7614-0817-7
1. United States—History—Civil War, 1861-1865—Causes—Juvenile literature.
2. United States—Politics and government—1815-1861—Juvenile literature.
[1. United States—History—1815-1861. 2. United States—History—Civil War,
1861-1865—Causes. 3. Slavery—History.]   I. Collier, James Lincoln, date.
II. Title. III. Series: Collier, Christopher, date. Drama of American history.
E459.C635 2000   98-2620
973.7'11—dc21   CIP
                                                      AC

Printed in Italy

3 5 6 4 2

CONTENTS

Over many years of both teaching and writing for students at all levels, from grammar school to graduate school, it has been borne in on us that many, if not most, American history textbooks suffer from trying to include everything of any moment in the history of the nation. Students become lost in a swamp of factual information, and as a consequence lose track of how those facts fit together and why they are significant and relevant to the world today.

In this series, our effort has been to strip the vast amount of available detail down to a central core. Our aim is to draw in bold strokes, providing enough information, but no more than is necessary, to bring out the basic themes of the American story, and what they mean to us now. We believe that it is surely more important for students to grasp the underlying concepts and ideas that emerge from the movement of history, than to memorize an array of facts and figures.

The difference between this series and many standard texts lies in what has been left out. We are convinced that students will better remember the important themes if they are not buried under a heap of names, dates, and places.

In this sense, our primary goal is what might be called citizenship education. We think it is critically important for America as a nation and Americans as individuals to understand the origins and workings of the public institutions that are central to American society. We have asked ourselves again and again what is most important for citizens of our democracy to know so they can most effectively make the system work for them and the nation. For this reason, we have focused on political and institutional history, leaving social and cultural history less well developed.

This series is divided into volumes that move chronologically through the American story. Each is built around a single topic, such as the Pilgrims, the Constitutional Convention, or immigration. Each volume has been written so that it can stand alone, for students who wish to research a given topic. As a consequence, in many cases material from previous volumes is repeated, usually in abbreviated form, to set the topic in its historical context. That is to say, students of the Constitutional Convention must be given some idea of relations with England, and why the Revolution was fought, even though the material was covered in detail in a previous volume. Readers should find that each volume tells an entire story that can be read with or without reference to other volumes.

Despite our belief that it is of the first importance to outline sharply basic concepts and generalizations, we have not neglected the great dramas of American history. The stories that will hold the attention of students are here, and we believe they will help the concepts they illustrate to stick in their minds. We think, for example, that knowing of Abraham Baldwin's brave and dramatic decision to vote with the small states at the Constitutional Convention will bring alive the Connecticut Compromise, out of which grew the American Senate.

Each of these volumes has been read by esteemed specialists in its particular topic; we have benefited from their comments.

CHAPTER I

The Slave Trade

The Civil War has continued to fascinate Americans generations after the people who fought it are long dead. No event in American history has been so thoroughly studied, not merely by historians, but by tens of thousands of other Americans who have made the war their hobby. Perhaps a hundred thousand books have been published about the Civil War: you could spend a lifetime just reading about the three days of the Battle of Gettysburg alone. Every year millions of Americans visit Civil War battlefields—Appomatox, Manassas, Gettysburg, and others. Scores of movies and television shows have re-created the battles, the personalities of the politicians and warriors who fought it. It was at once a great drama and a fearful tragedy, which cost the lives of 620,000 Americans, mostly young men and even boys of fourteen and fifteen. What was the reason for this frightful carnage?

Historians started arguing over the causes of the Civil War almost from the moment it started and have gone on arguing ever since. Many different interpretations have been offered. Some historians have argued that the war was mainly about money matters and economic power—the South was jealous of Northern wealth and was afraid of being buried by its richer neighbor. Others have pointed to slavery: one important historian has said that slavery was "the sole cause of the war," and added, "If the Negro had never been brought to America, our Civil War could not have occurred." Though there are a number of other important interpretations, that slavery was the central cause of the war is the one that is emphasized in this volume. Despite our emphasis on slavery, we will remind readers from time to time of the political, economic, and cultural differences that divided the North and South. In order to understand both how and why the United States was torn apart in this terrible, bloody struggle, we need to stand back a little, and see how passions on both sides of the line rose step by step until the war became inevitable.

Regional differences in culture and economy due to climate, topography, and the attitudes of the settlers showed up right from the start of colonization in the seventeenth century. Thus it was clear, from the moment that the new nation was formed after 1776, that the two sections of the country were natural rivals. Their climates were different, the type of farming they did was different, they followed different economies, and had differing ways of life. But as James Madison said at the Constitutional Convention in 1787, "The states were divided into different interests . . . principally from . . . their having or not having slaves." In Madison's view, slavery itself produced a lot of the other differences between the two sections of the nation. How did slavery come to play so crucial a role?

Slavery was by no means an American invention. It has existed in many times and places over the long history of humankind. Indeed, it is probable that most human societies have had slavery in some form or other. Forms of human exploitation resembling slavery are still practiced today in some parts of the world.

Slavery existed in Africa before the coming of Europeans. That vast continent was home to a very diverse group of people—probably, by the 1400s, as diverse a population as existed anywhere in the world. It

The North and South, almost from the beginning of the settlement of what would be the United States, were natural rivals. The South depended mainly on agriculture for its income. The picture above shows a typical small Southern farm of the 1600s, in a re-creation at Jamestown, Virginia. By contrast, the North developed a thriving commercial trade, selling goods to the Caribbean Islands, Europe, even Asia, as well as at home. At right, a view of Philadelphia in the 1700s, showing its busy harbor.

included some of the tallest human beings, like the Masai, and some of the shortest, like the Pygmies. They ranged in skin color from very dark to tan. They spoke hundreds of languages and dialects of those languages, followed a variety of religions, had differing diets and ways of getting food.

Most of the slaves brought to America came from West Africa, where today lie the countries of Senegal, Guinea, Congo, Benin, Nigeria, and Angola—the part of Africa closest to the Americas. The people in this area lived mainly in small, self-contained villages, usually surrounded by fields and gardens where the villagers grew their crops and herded their cattle, sheep, and goats.

These villages were often organized into loose alliances of people speaking the same language. Such little kingdoms at times grew into more formidable ones. At the time of the first European voyages to Africa, the kingdom of Benin was large, prosperous, and dominated many of the groups in the surrounding area. The first European explorer, a Portuguese trader named Ruy de Sequeiria who arrived in Benin in 1472, was forced to throw himself down before a king who wore so much gold jewelry on his arms that he needed servants to raise them up.

West Africa was by no means a primitive place. It contained large towns where craftsmen smelted brass, iron, and gold, carved elaborate statues, built furniture inlaid with ivory and precious stones. Townsmen traded across the region and into eastern and northern Africa to places thousands of miles away. Timbuktu, the capital city of the Mali empire, was for hundreds of years a great trading center. In the 1300s there was a Mohammedan university in Timbuktu not unlike those in Europe.

But despite a few great cities and empires that rose and fell, life for most West Africans centered on their villages. Children grew up following traditional daily rituals, worked in the fields, fished in the seas and rivers.

Slavery was commonplace in West Africa. People who owed money sometimes became slaves to satisfy their debts; a whole family might be enslaved for the husband and father's debts. During times of famine people might sell themselves or their children into slavery to get something to eat. Some slaves were criminals, who were enslaved as punishment for their crimes. Children left at home to play while the villagers went off to work the fields were sometimes kidnapped by slavers from other villages.

But the largest number of slaves were prisoners of war. In fact, some wars were started by one group for the specific purpose of taking slaves, who could then be sold or traded within or among the villages—and in time to Europeans—at a considerable profit.

To be torn away from family and friends to live among strangers was a ghastly misery, especially for a child kidnapped from a village. But slaves in Africa were not usually treated as badly as they would be in

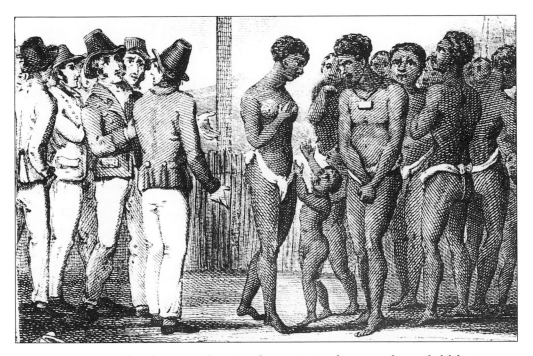

This engraving of a slave market, made in 1810, shows a slave child being separated from its parents as a result of a sale.

A slave pen in Alexandria, Virginia, where slaves were held until they could be sold. Many, including Southerners who accepted slavery, believed that the slave trade—the buying and selling of human beings—was particularly evil.

America. They were slaves, of course, and might be confined or tied up if they tried to run away. But otherwise they lived much as the villagers did, performing routine tasks, and even eating and sleeping with the family that owned them.

Paradoxically, considering how things turned out, the custom of slavery that existed in Africa and elsewhere, did not then exist in most of Europe. The Spanish and Portuguese who fought and traded with the Moors of North Africa sometimes enslaved Moorish prisoners of war (and Moors, as well as Turks, in turn enslaved European travelers and shipwrecked sailors). But the English, who would be the primary settlers of what would become the United States, had had no slavery at home since the thirteenth century, three hundred years before colonization. Yet it would be the English colonists who brought slavery to the area that one day would become the United States.

The path to transatlantic slavery began in the 1400s, before Europeans knew that anything like the Americas existed. At that time the Portuguese in particular, who were great sailors, were exploring down the West Coast of Africa, and up rivers there, in order to trade for ivory, gold, and other precious items. They also began trading for the slaves whom many Africans, especially kings and chieftains, held. These slaves were brought back to Spain, Portugal and elsewhere to act as laborers and house servants. Thus slavery was imported into Europe from Africa.

In 1492 Columbus made his famous landfall on a Caribbean island. Very quickly thereafter the Spanish and Portuguese began conquering the Indians of the Caribbean, Central America, Mexico, and large portions of South America. They were not interested in colonizing the area, but in wresting from it gold, silver, precious jewels, and valuable timber like mahogany. American Indians had used prisoners of war as slaves to work the gold and silver mines. The Europeans continued the system, enslaving thousands of Indians to work the mines and do other menial tasks.

But the Indians proved to be poor slaves when working under the Spanish lash. Large numbers of Indians died of diseases the Europeans brought in, diseases like smallpox, measles, and yellow fever. Others grew ill from the effects of slavery, to the point where whole groups, like the Arawaks of the Caribbean, died out completely.

By this time, the middle of the 1500s, the Spanish and Portuguese were beginning to grow large quantities of crops, particularly sugar and tobacco, that brought extremely good prices in Europe. The European masters needed thousands of workers to cultivate these crops. As the Indians did not make productive slaves, plantation owners turned to Africa, where there existed a ready supply of people already enslaved or liable to be.

Unfortunately, Africans who owned slaves, especially kings and chieftains who owned a lot of them, were quite willing to trade them for European products like textiles, guns, swords, tools, liquor, and orna-

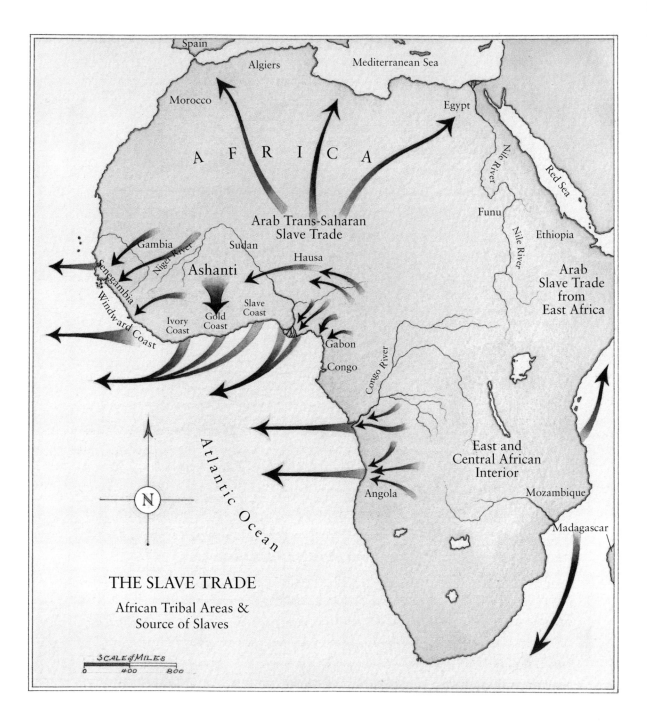

THE SLAVE TRADE

African Tribal Areas &
Source of Slaves

SCALE of MILES

0   400   800

The death rate for slaves was high, especially in the states of the lower South. As this advertisement of a slave auction in South Carolina shows, small-pox was a particularly dangerous disease for whites and blacks alike.

TO BE SOLD, on board the Ship *Bance-Island*, on tuesday the 6th of *May* next, at *Aſhley-Ferry*; a choice cargo of about 250 fine healthy

NEGROES,

juſt arrived from the Windward & Rice Coaſt.
——The utmoſt care has already been taken, and ſhall be continued, to keep them free from the leaſt danger of being infected with the SMALL-POX, no boat having been on board, and all other communication with people from *Charles-Town* prevented.

Auſtin, Laurens, & Appleby.

N. B. Full one Half of the above Negroes have had the SMALL-POX in their own Country.

ments. The slave trade operated in a variety of ways. However, most commonly, Europeans slavers built forts (called "factories") on the West African coast, usually where rivers came from the interior down to the sea. The English, French, Spanish, and Portuguese all had such factories. Slaves were brought into these forts by their African captors or traders to be sold. Sometimes, after a war, the victorious African king would bring in a hundred or more prisoners of war. Slave ships from the various nations would sail to their own forts and pick up the slaves who were being held there.

Such ships, when crammed full, might carry as many as six hundred people at a time, although usually cargoes were smaller than this. Frequently there would not be enough captives in the fort, or factory, and the ship would have to wait there for weeks, or even months, while enough slaves to make a cargo were collected.

Far and away the largest number of these African slaves were brought

An artist's conception of slaves being stowed in the infamous cramped lower decks of a slave ship. This illustration was taken from a book published in the 1800s.

to South America and the Caribbean—about ninety percent, according to one historian. Over the whole period of the transatlantic slave trade more than three and a half million went to Brazil, for instance, and over a million and a half went to the British West Indies. Only about five percent of the enslaved Africans—about 275,000—were brought to the English colonies that would become the United States. By the 1600s the English, as we have seen, had not practiced slavery for at least three centuries, and English colonists were slow to adopt it. Slavery never became widespread north of Delaware, although it did exist in every English American colony.

Though sugar was the principal slave-produced crop elsewhere, what really brought massive slavery to mainland North America was tobacco. The first of the English colonies, at Jamestown, Virginia, struggled mightily to survive from the time it was founded in 1607. In about 1615, the colonists discovered a type of tobacco that would grow well there. Within two or three years, the Virginia colony was beginning to make substantial profits from tobacco. Land in the colony was cheap—there were millions of acres that could be bought for almost nothing. If you could get hold of some land and grow tobacco on it you could make a lot of money, even become rich. But you needed people to work the land. Indentured servants—people who signed contracts to work for a stipulated period, usually about seven years—mostly teen-age boys off the streets of English cities, died of local diseases at such a rate that labor was always in short supply. Though the first Africans came to Virginia in 1619, wide-scale adoption of slavery did not occur till nearly fifty years later. But by 1670 Virginians were fully committed to a system of black chattel slavery. (Chattels are personal property. For the story of how slavery developed in Virginia see *The Paradox of Jamestown* in this series.)

The first Africans to arrive in North America were not usually treated as harshly as black slaves would be later. Some were treated as indentured servants, who were freed after serving for a number of years. Others were kept as slaves for life. Unaccustomed to slavery, Virginians were not quite sure how it should work. But as the years passed, and more and more slaves were brought in to work the tobacco plantations, the system of slavery grew harder and more rigid. By 1700 there was no longer any question of blacks being treated as servants. They were now seen as subhuman, to be trained to obey and worked as hard as possible. They were frequently whipped, fed rough diets consisting of corn and pork, and given worn clothing to wear.

Colonists in New England and other northern ports, although they

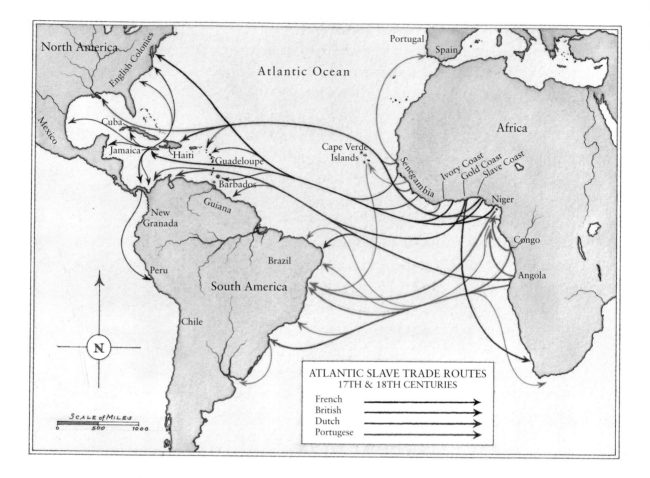

ATLANTIC SLAVE TRADE ROUTES
17TH & 18TH CENTURIES

French	→
British	→
Dutch	→
Portugese	→

kept relatively few slaves, played a major role in establishing slavery. The American shipping industry lay in the North, and it was northern shippers, sea captains, and merchants who carried on the slave trade with Africa, of course along with slavers from Portugal, France, Holland, and England. In time a notorious triangular trade developed. On the first leg of the trip, ships would carry New England rum and other goods like muskets to Africa to trade for slaves. On the third leg the ships would bring back to New England molasses from the Caribbean (made from sugar cane) to be distilled into more rum. It was the second leg of the trip, the "middle passage," from the West Coast of Africa to the Americas, with ships jammed with black slaves, that has become infamous.

The treatment of the slaves during the middle passage was so cruel that it is hard to believe that humans would treat other humans that way. During the daytime, when the weather was good, the slaves, a few at a time, were usually allowed up on deck shackled together in pairs. At night they were crammed into tiny spaces below deck, sometimes so tightly packed that they had to sleep pressed against one another like nests of spoons. In many of these ships they slept on platforms so close above one another that they could not sit up. Many of the slaves became sick, and probably 10 percent or 15 percent of them died during the trip. The stench in the slave quarters was terrible, especially during storms when the windows had to be sealed.

Some captains of slave ships sailing the middle passage believed that the slaves ought to be treated as well as possible under such conditions: each healthy slave was worth a good deal more in the American slave markets than a sick one. A dead one was worth nothing at all. Such captains tried to feed the slaves enough to keep them in good health. They would bring them on deck for fresh air as much as possible, and sometimes make them sing and dance to keep their spirits up. Some captains even had doctors on board to care for ill slaves. But others had a different idea, which was that a certain number of slaves would die anyway, and there was no point in wasting money on anything beyond minimum care for them.

On occasion captives rebelled, especially when the ships were anchored off the African coast collecting slaves. Some of these rebellions succeeded, but most were put down by the sailors fighting with guns and swords against unarmed slaves. Some blacks decided they would rather die if they could not be free and managed to jump overboard and drown themselves. Others tried to starve themselves to death. In a few cases captives actually ripped open their flesh with their fingernails in order to

Revulsion against slavery grew steadily in many places. England outlawed it long before the American Civil War, and thereafter used its navy to halt slave ships as they left Africa. Here an Arab slave ship raises its sail to escape an approaching British naval ship that can be seen distantly at the left of the picture.

bleed to death. But in fact, the number of African prisoners who committed suicide during the middle passage was small. Most of them lived to suffer for weeks or even months on the middle passage and to be sold into slavery in the Americas.

Today we find it very difficult to understand how human beings could treat other people in such a cruel fashion. We should realize that back in the 1500s and 1600s, people had less respect for human life than we do today. Masters were frequently cruel to their servants of any race or nation; harsh treatment was expected as the normal thing. But clearly, Europeans saw blacks as very different from themselves. They did not believe that blacks could reason as they did, were not as sensitive to pain, were not as capable of affection, grief, loyalty, and comradeship as whites were.

Today we understand that people of all races and ethnic groups are basically much the same in their feelings and the things that concern them. Human joys and sorrows are similar in people everywhere. But that was not so well understood in the sixteenth and seventeenth centuries. Among other things, different races and ethnic groups had far less contact with each other than they do in the United States today. Whatever the case, in that era many, if not most, Europeans were able to treat blacks with a cruelty they would rarely inflict on other whites.

CHAPTER II

The Slave South

Few topics in American history have been written about with such passion as Southern slavery. Our picture of it has been formed mainly by works like the novels *Gone with the Wind* and *Uncle Tom's Cabin*, both immensely popular, written by authors with special points of view. Among such works are many movies, books, and television shows that show slavery at its worst, the slaves incessantly whipped and tortured. There is an equally great pile of material that pretends that slavery was benign and the slaveholders were always kind to their slaves. What, exactly, is the truth?

To begin with, about three-quarters of all Southern families did not own any slaves at all. The ordinary Southerner was a small farmer who raised enough corn and hogs to feed his family, and grew some cotton or tobacco for the market, with the help of his sons and daughters and perhaps a hired hand or two. Of those families that did own slaves, half owned fewer than five, and almost three-quarters fewer than ten. The huge plantations, with thousands of acres worked by hundreds of slaves, which we so often think of as typical of that day, were relatively rare; the majority of slaves were held on middle-sized plantations worked by twenty to a hundred slaves. On one large plantation there were 135 slaves, big and little, the overseer there explained, "of which sixty-seven went to the field regularly. . . . Besides the field hands, there were . . . a blacksmith, carpenter and wheelwright, two seamstresses, one cook, one table servant, the overseer's house servant, one midwife and nurse." A list, we should note, that includes seven or eight skilled laborers.

Furthermore, by the middle of the nineteenth century, the bulk of slaves lived on farms and plantations in the Deep South, especially South Carolina, Georgia, Mississippi, Florida, and Alabama. The border states,

We tend to think of slavery in terms of white-porticoed mansions and hundreds of slaves toiling in vast fields, but in fact three-quarters of slaveholders had fewer than ten. The plantation shown here, with a few slaves working a modest acreage, is more typical.

such as Kentucky, Maryland, and Missouri, had proportionately far fewer slaves. Virginia and North Carolina had a surplus that they were selling to plantation owners in the Deep South. Indeed, one feature of slavery in America that set it off from other places was the high fertility rate. Where Caribbean plantations had constantly to replenish their supply of slaves from Africa, blacks in the United States had large families and lived longer lives, so that by the 1830s most of them were generations removed from Africa.

Plantation slaves worked from sunup to dark, in the summer as long as sixteen hours, with only enough time off at noon to eat a midday meal in the fields. Of course, many white folks worked that long, too, but the work week amounted to one and a half to two times the forty-hour week Americans consider normal today.

The standard diet was three pounds of bacon or pork and about twelve quarts of cornmeal a week per person. Often the slaves were able to supplement this with green vegetables grown in their own plots and sometimes with possum and other wild animal meat.

Of course, slaves had no motivation to work since work got nothing for themselves. Despite incentives like a promise of time off, they contrived many clever ways to slow down or avoid work altogether, such as deliberately breaking tools, and faking illness or injury. Thus plantation owners figured that slaves did only about two-thirds as much work in a day as laborers—black and white—who were paid a wage.

It is probable that on the small plantations with only a handful of slaves, those slaves fared better than on the larger plantations. Farm families with only a few slaves often worked alongside them in the fields, simply because every hand was needed to cultivate the crops. Such white families would establish personal relationships with their slaves, which might make the slaves' lives easier. But it is nonetheless true that most slaveholders believed that blacks would not work at all, and certainly not efficiently, if they were not taught to fear punishment. Slaveholders had various ways of punishing blacks, such as locking them up alone, or putting them in stocks, just the same as white criminals were. But they had come to believe that the most effective weapon was the lash. To be sure, some slaveholders disliked whipping their slaves, and did it rarely.

Slave cabins were usually made of logs, with the whole family or frequently several families, sharing one or two rooms. Cooking was done in a fireplace. To the left of the cabin is a portion of fence, which surrounded a small garden slaves were sometimes allowed to keep in their spare time, to grow extra vegetables for their own use, or to earn a few pennies.

Others felt it was important for slaves to get a taste of the lash occasionally just to remind them of what it felt like. Some plantation masters were simply cruel and lashed their slaves at the slightest excuse or for no reason at all. A practiced hand with the lash could rip open the flesh, and the backs of some slaves, especially those of a rebellious temperament, were a mass of scar tissue.

Particularly prone to lash the slaves were the overseers who managed the larger plantations. Overseers went out to the fields with the hands, often on horseback, and would strike out with the lash when they felt a slave was not working hard enough. Many of them prided themselves on their ability to keep their slaves in line and took it as a duty to

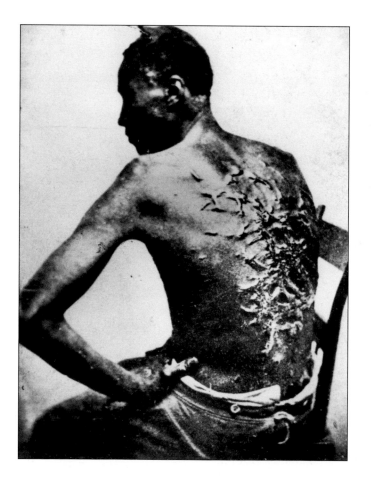

Not every slaveowner was cruel, and not all of them beat their slaves regularly. But nearly all of them used the lash from time to time to command obedience from the slaves, and some used the lash frequently, as the scars on this slave's back clearly show.

lash for small infractions of the rule. There are cases of slaveholders firing their overseers because they were too quick with the lash. In fact, slaves were sometimes beaten to death by overseers or even masters—though usually unintentionally, for slaves were expensive to replace.

However, despite the lash, probably the greatest pain the slaves suffered was psychological and emotional. They knew they had little chance to escape, although probably many lived with that hope. They were always and forever at the mercy of somebody else, always had to do what they were told, were never able to make a free decision for themselves. It is true that most blacks were able to maneuver things one way or another to make the best of their situations. They usually had Sundays off and generally a few days at Christmastime. Some were able to hire themselves out on their free time to make a little money, and a tiny few even saved enough in this way to buy their freedom. Others managed to escape and make their way north. Blacks had their lives apart from their masters, their times of song and dance, their moments of laughter, their private jokes at the expense of the whites. In their little cabins they cooked, reared their children, and carried on as best they could the activities customary in families everywhere. But always there was that huge hand over them holding them down, and they hated it.

Particularly painful for blacks was the experience of being sold away from their families and the plantations where they had grown up. Sometimes a master would sell a slave because the slave was difficult to manage, but most sales took place when an owner needed money for some reason, or when the master died and his heirs did not want to continue the plantation. Husbands were sold away from wives, mothers were sold away from their children, and brothers and sisters sold away from each other. It was, of course, a searing sorrow for parents and children to part in this way, knowing that it was very unlikely they would ever see each other again.

So much has been written about the evils of slavery in the South that we often forget that in the eighteenth and nineteenth centuries tens of thousands of blacks lived in the North as well. Some of these had recently come north, having escaped from slavery or having bought their freedom. Most, however, had been there for generations. Beginning in the 1630s there were black slaves in all northern colonies, and slavery was still legal in some of them as late as the 1840s. William Samuel Johnson, a delegate to the Constitutional Convention from Connecticut, owned several slaves, and sixty years after the U.S. Constitution was written, slavery was still legal in Connecticut. Pennsylvania never officially ended slavery, but the institution died out in the face of hostile public opinion and inhibiting legislation. There were always far fewer slaves in the North than in the South.

The attitude toward blacks in the North was very mixed. Quakers in Germantown, Pennsylvania, took a stand against slavery as early as 1688. In 1700 the Puritan judge Samuel Sewall wrote a pamphlet against slavery, a practice he did not believe could be justified in a Christian community. Indeed, the conflict between the principles of Christianity and the practice of slavery created tensions within individual Americans and in American society until the end of the Civil War.

Nonetheless, it is also true that as late as the early 1800s, probably the majority of Northerners were indifferent to the whole question. It did not touch most of them directly. Slavery was either abolished or in the process of gradual abolition in all the states north of Delaware. But in fact, many, and perhaps most, Northerners agreed with Southerners that blacks were an inferior people, simple and lazy, who were unfit for anything but the roughest kind of work. Even many people who opposed slavery for religious or philosophical reasons believed that blacks were inferior. In truth, until after the Civil War, the number of people in the North who wanted to give blacks full rights as citizens was minute. Even free blacks could not vote, eat and sleep in inns with whites, join the militia, or sit alongside whites in church. In most states it was illegal for blacks and whites to marry. In other states it was simply assumed that most whites would not want to associate with blacks.

Given this attitude, it is not surprising that the Founding Fathers of the Revolutionary era, so eager for freedom from England for themselves, did not seriously consider giving the same freedom to African-Americans. In an early draft of the Declaration of Independence, Thomas Jefferson characterized the slave trade as "this execrable commerce." But no references to the trade appeared in the final draft. And, of course, a large proportion of the authors of the Declaration of Independence, the Constitution, and the Bill of Rights owned slaves.

Nonetheless, all over America during the era of the Revolution the cry for freedom was heard, and it is not surprising that blacks heard it, too. Scores of northern blacks singly and in groups petitioned state legislatures for an end to slavery and for equal rights. During the Revolution some blacks in Connecticut (where slavery was not legally abolished until 1848) wrote in a petition, "We hope that our good mistress, the free state of Connecticut, engaged in a war against tyranny, will not sell good honest [black patriots] and friends of freedom, as we are."

A few whites saw the justice in this. One was "astonished to see a people eager for liberty holding Negroes in bondage." The contradiction was plain. But even so, when the Constitution was being written, the delegates did not seriously consider trying to end slavery. Even a few of the Southern delegates to the Constitutional Convention, like George Mason, disliked slavery but understood that the delegates from the Carolinas and Georgia would walk out if the Convention tried to tamper with slavery. Beyond that, no one could figure out a way to end it, anyway. The Convention delegates believed it was more important for them to put together the new nation than it was to solve the difficult problem of slavery. After much compromise, the Constitution said that the new United States government could, if it wanted to, abolish the importation of new slaves after twenty years; that masters could chase and recapture

Even some Southerners disliked slavery, and wanted to put an end to it. George Mason, a Virginian who wrote a Bill of Rights for his state, opposed slavery, but at the Constitutional Convention of 1787, he knew that delegates from the lower South would leave if the Convention tried to abolish slavery. Like some other delegates, he felt he had to accept slavery to create a workable United States.

runaway slaves who had fled into Northern states; and that in figuring out representation in Congress, three-fifths of the slaves would be counted. But the basic underlying message was that slavery was to be permitted in states that wanted it—that is to say, the Southern states. The right to keep slaves, then, had the authority of the Constitution behind it. (The Constitutional Convention of 1787 is described in the volume of The Drama of American History called *Creating the Constitution*.)

But there was a joker in the deck: What about slavery in new states? When the Constitution was written in 1787, most of the population of the United States lived in the area between the Atlantic Ocean and the formidable Appalachian mountain chain, about a hundred miles inland. Beyond the Appalachians lay an immense amount of fertile land inhabited largely by Indians. Various states had claims to the land across the Appalachians, and by 1787 Americans were beginning to drift into the

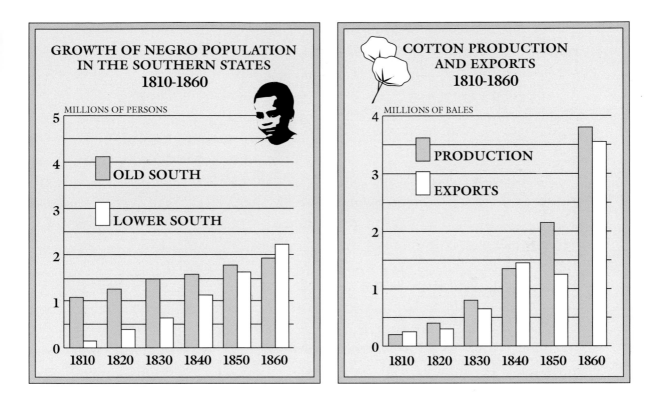

GROWTH OF NEGRO POPULATION IN THE SOUTHERN STATES 1810-1860

MILLIONS OF PERSONS

OLD SOUTH

LOWER SOUTH

5 4 3 2 1 0

1810 1820 1830 1840 1850 1860

COTTON PRODUCTION AND EXPORTS 1810-1860

MILLIONS OF BALES

PRODUCTION

EXPORTS

4 3 2 1 0

1810 1820 1830 1840 1850 1860

area to hunt, trap, trade, and carve farms out of the wilderness. It was clear that this land would eventually be settled, and brought in as states. So at the same time that the Constitutional Convention was meeting in Philadelphia, the old Congress meeting in New York reached yet one more compromise between North and South called the Northwest Ordinance: Slavery would be prohibited in the so-called Northwest Territory, the land lying between the Ohio and the Mississippi Rivers north to the Canadian border, which was under the authority of Congress. Nothing was said about the land *south* of the Ohio, which was still part of Virginia, North Carolina, and Georgia, but the understanding was that slavery would be allowed there.

This seemed to settle matters. Most people believed that it would be a long time before the vast Northwest Territory would be settled. In the meanwhile, many Northerners believed, the importation of new slaves would have stopped, and slavery would die a natural death.

But events, as they often do, took charge. For one thing, the invention of the cotton gin in 1793 made cotton plantations vastly more efficient and profitable. The demand for slaves in the Deep South grew rapidly. Between 1790 and 1820 the number of slaves in the United States more than doubled, to over one and a half million. For another thing, in 1803 President Jefferson bought from France the huge Louisiana Territory, larger than many European nations. It ran west from the Mississippi River to the Rocky Mountains, from the Canadian border south to the Gulf of Mexico east of the Arkansas River. That is, it did not include Texas and what is now Arizona and New Mexico. Once again, it was assumed that it would be centuries before this new land was filled with Americans. But in fact Americans had already, before the Louisiana Purchase, been slipping across the Mississippi into the Louisiana Territory to hunt, trap, and even start farming. The trickle became a stream, and by 1810 it was clear that people out there across the Mississippi would soon be clamoring to join the United States. And would these new states be slave or free?

The issue was forced to the surface in Missouri. As early as 1810, only seven years after the Louisiana Purchase, there were 16,000 whites and four thousand blacks in the territory. Ten years later there were 56,000 whites and 11,000 blacks. Missouri was slave territory whether anyone liked it or not. According to the Northwest Ordinance, a territory could apply for statehood when it had a population of 60,000. By 1819 Missouri had 56,000 free whites and it applied to Congress for statehood. When the elderly former president Thomas Jefferson heard of this his heart sank. "This momentous question, like a fireball in the night, awakened and filled me with terror," he said. Jefferson was not alone in his foreboding. Soon-to-be president John Quincy Adams described the

Missouri question as "a title page to a great tragic volume." The debate in Congress was ferocious. Most Northern congressmen were determined that Missouri come in only as a free state. Suddenly the slavery issue, which had been so adroitly buried at the Constitutional Convention and kept under wraps by cooperating congressmen for a generation, was out in the open.

Southerners felt betrayed. Since the signing of the Constitution, it had been understood that nobody's slaves would be taken away from them. If Missouri came in as a free state, slaveholders there would lose their slaves. Wasn't a central purpose of any government to protect private property? Didn't the U.S. Government have a moral duty to do so? Didn't the Fifth Amendment to the Constitution say specifically that nobody's property could be taken away from them without due process of law?

Debate was bitter and prolonged. The more populous North had the majority in the House of Representatives, but the Senate was divided equally, and senators effectively could prevent laws they didn't like from being passed. Congress was deadlocked. Maine was also seeking admission—as a free state; but the Senate would not let it come in unless Missouri was admitted as a slave state.

Finally the Kentucky statesman, Henry Clay, worked out a compromise and made an impassioned speech in which he called upon his fellow congressmen to listen to reason. In the end a compromise was agreed upon: Missouri would come in as a slave state, but a line would be drawn through the Louisiana Purchase territory at 36°30'—the southern border of Missouri—north of which no more slave states would be admitted, except of course Missouri. Maine would come in as a free state at the same time.

But hardly had an agreement been reached, when the citizens of Missouri upended it, by putting into their constitution a clause prohibiting free blacks and mulattos from entering the state. This was contrary

Henry Clay, senator from Kentucky, was one of the most celebrated politicians of the time, and very influential in Congress. He was mainly responsible for maneuvering the Missouri Compromise through Congress, and for the moment staving off a split in the Union.

to the national constitution, which said explicitly that a citizen of any state was entitled to the "privileges and immunities" of any other state. In places like Massachusetts there were free blacks who were citizens of the state. By rights, they should be allowed to enter Missouri.

Clay went back to work and found another compromise: Congress would accept the Missouri clause, but only if no law would discriminate against citizens of other states. The statement was perhaps meaningless because many people believed that African Americans were not—and could not be—citizens. But it was accepted, and once more the slavery issue had been ducked.

Most Northerners felt that the South had really won on the issue: after all, there would be slavery in Missouri, which was the key point. Many Southerners were also unhappy about the Missouri Compromise, for they felt that the Constitution permitted slaveholders to take their slaves anywhere: the issue should never have come up. But more and more people in the North—and some in the South, too—were becoming deeply committed to ending slavery everywhere in the United States. They especially wanted to prevent its expansion into new territories. On both sides determination was stiffening. Lines were being drawn in the dirt.

We can understand why Southerners felt so strongly about slavery. For many, their wealth and their high social status depended upon keeping the whole system of slavery going. Moreover, it is human nature for people to hate being at the bottom of the social heap. Poor whites in the South scratching out meager livings in small farms in the hills—and there were plenty of them—knew they could never be at the bottom as long as there were black slaves below them. Probably few of them thought this through, but they felt it all the same.

The hardening attitude against slavery in the North is more difficult to understand. Previously, the majority of Northerners had not cared much about slavery one way or another, although probably most of them would have admitted that they thought it was wrong, or unchristian. Moreover, at the time of the Missouri Compromise in 1820 most Northerners thought that blacks were an inferior people and did not want to associate with them. And yet, by 1861, so many would come to feel so strongly about slavery that they would be willing to see their fathers, husbands, and sons march off to be slaughtered by the tens of thousands to end slavery. How did this dramatic change of attitude come about?

There had always been at least a few Americans who disapproved of slavery. Many of them were in New England, where religion was strong, and the buying and selling of human beings like cattle seemed unchristian. But undoubtedly the strongest force against slavery were the Quakers. Pennsylvania had been founded as a haven for the Quaker faith, which had been illegal in England. But there were Quakers in many other states, too. As early as 1688 Quakers were talking against slavery. In 1744 a rule was adopted under which a Quaker could be expelled for buying and selling slaves. By the 1780s there had been created the Pennsylvania Abolition Society, which served as a model for abolition societies in other states. Although non-Quakers joined these societies, the bulk of the members were Quakers.

Quakers, however, were not alone in creating a rising demand in the North for abolition of slavery. Beginning in the 1820s, there had been in the United States and parts of Europe a growing interest in reform. At the time, Americans by and large had been quite easygoing about sex, had drunk a great deal more alcohol than we do today, and were casual about religion: some of our early presidents, like Thomas Jefferson, did not really believe in God as presented in the Bible.

In the 1820s a lot of people decided that it was time for the country to return to the old religious values that—as they saw it—the nation had been founded on. Along with this religious revival came demands for reforms in many areas—a general cleaning-up of the society. A very strong "temperance" movement arose to curb, or even eliminate, the drinking of alcohol. A women's movement also grew, demanding more rights for women, who at the time could not vote, hold office, or join the professions. People like Horace Mann began working to improve public education, in part to make sure that boys would grow up to be intelligent voters. New ideas about how to reform criminals took hold: prisons would no longer simply punish people, but would attempt to make criminals better people. A lot of "utopian" communities, meant to create small idealistic societies, were started. Many of these reform movements swept the South as well as the North: the Southern religious revival meetings were famous, and the temperance movement against alcohol was strong in the South, too.

But there was another element in this reformist wave that was not popular in the South, and that was the growing cry for the abolition of

The movement in the North to end slavery was part of the rise of a new morality that grew up from about 1820 on. Important to this movement was a revival of interest in religious "camp meetings," which went on for days, and were common in both North and South. Top, a tent camp of people gathering near Hartford, Connecticut, to hear a charismatic religious leader preach. At right, a man caught up in the religious fervor typical of such meetings.

slavery. Slavery just did not seem to agree with Christian ideas of tolerance and love for your fellow humans. And as more and more people were swept up by the religious revival, they were forced to face this issue: could they be good Christians and still support slavery? In the South they thought they could; certain parts of the Bible seemed to accept slavery. But in the North more and more people began to believe that they must oppose it.

Yet many of these same whites who were against slavery were not really eager to have blacks sitting beside them on church pews or voting at the polls for mayors or representatives in Congress. For these people, one good solution was to free blacks and ship them back to Africa to establish colonies there. In 1815 a black shipowner, Paul Cuffee, at his own expense transported thirty-eight blacks to Africa. Whites were attracted to this idea and formed the American Colonization Society, which in 1822 founded the colony of Liberia on the West Coast of Africa. As many people saw

A silhouette of the wealthy black shipowner and merchant, Paul Cuffee, who organized the immigration of some American blacks to Africa. Silhouettes of this kind, often cut or torn from a piece of paper, were a popular form of portraiture at the time.

it, blacks would never really be accepted in the United States. The free blacks in the North often lived in slum conditions, and worked at the lowest jobs, for the lowest pay. Surely they would be happier elsewhere, these reformers thought. By 1860 only 2,638 blacks had agreed to go to Liberia. That, of course, was a tiny drop in the bucket of about two and a half million African Americans in the United States in 1840. Indeed, it was about the same number of African Americans born here every three months.

Most blacks, obviously, disliked the whole idea. For better or worse they were Americans, born and bred. They were no more familiar with African ways and the African countryside than were whites. Some white abolitionists agreed with them. They felt that rather than ship the blacks away, it was up to whites to make room in American society for them. In the end, the colonization idea, although quite popular for a time, never produced great results. Clearly, colonizationists had no feelings of equality for Africans. For them antislavery was a matter of what was good for white Americans. Most Northerners by the 1830s opposed slavery on moral, religious, or policy grounds, but very few believed in actually abolishing slavery. They could live with it if they had to.

But some white Americans had come to hate slavery on the basis of their own moral convictions. One of the most important of these was William Lloyd Garrison, who thought that the African colonization scheme was racist. He founded a newspaper called *The Liberator* to spread his abolitionist ideas. In 1833 Garrison joined with others to found the American Anti-Slavery Society, which attempted to coordinate the activities of many state and local abolitionist societies. Eventually such organizations had 200,000 members.

One of the people influenced by Garrison's *The Liberator* was Frederick Douglass, perhaps the most influential African American of the nineteenth century. Douglass was born a slave in Maryland. His father was white, possibly his master. His mother died when he was young and

Frederick Douglass was the most celebrated black leader of his day. A former slave, he could speak with authority on the conditions endured by slaves, and attracted large audiences to his speeches and writings. Former slaves like Douglass were important in raising awareness in the North of the horrors of slavery, and increasing the pressure to end it.

he had only a few memories of her. Growing up, he was moved around frequently. Some of his owners were relatively kind, and through one of them he learned to read and write. But often they were extremely cruel: Douglass was whipped many times.

Once, when his master was trying to tie his legs so he could whip him, Douglass decided to fight back. "From whence came the spirit I don't know—I resolve to fight. . . . My resistance was so entirely unexpected that [the master] seemed taken all aback. He trembled like a leaf. This gave me assurance." In the end, the master did not beat him. Encouraged, Douglass eventually escaped into the North, where he came across *The Liberator*. He quickly involved himself in the abolitionist movement, becoming one of its most important spokespeople, an eloquent speaker and writer who greatly affected audiences.

People like Douglass and other escaped slaves were very important to the abolition movement, for they could testify from firsthand experience about the horrors of slavery. People who heard them speak could not go home still believing that slavery was a benign institution that protected slaves from themselves.

A stream of books and articles about slavery flooded the North in the years leading up to the Civil War. This picture from a book shows a slave auction. In the background is the Capitol Building with a flag over it saying, "All Men are Free and Equal," to drive the point home.

By no means did the abolition movement sweep up all Northerners, or even a majority of them. It was especially strong in New England and places like upstate New York to which many New Englanders had immigrated. It had pockets of strength elsewhere, especially among the Quakers. But in the big cities there was a good deal of opposition to abolitionism. Especially opposed were laboring people, particularly Irish and German immigrants, who feared that if blacks were raised to equality with them, the blacks might take their jobs.

The 200,000 active mem-bers of the abolitionist organizations were only a tiny proportion of the Northern population. But their influence was far greater than their numbers.

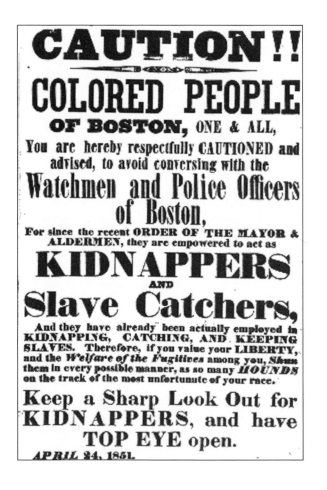

CAUTION!!

COLORED PEOPLE

OF BOSTON, ONE & ALL,

You are hereby respectfully CAUTIONED and advised, to avoid conversing with the

Watchmen and Police Officers of Boston,

For since the recent ORDER OF THE MAYOR & ALDERMEN, they are empowered to act as

KIDNAPPERS

AND

Slave Catchers,

And they have already been actually employed in KIDNAPPING, CATCHING, AND KEEPING SLAVES. Therefore, if you value your LIBERTY, and the Welfare of the Fugitives among you, Shun them in every possible manner, as so many HOUNDS on the track of the most unfortunate of your race.

Keep a Sharp Look Out for KIDNAPPERS, and have TOP EYE open.

APRIL 24, 1851.

By no means did all whites, even Northern whites, want to associate with blacks, or even care whether slavery was abolished or not. This poster, which was put around Boston, shows clearly that the city's officials were helping kidnappers to take blacks back into slavery. Returning runaway slaves was legal, but frequently these so-called slave catchers kidnapped free blacks who had never been slaves and hauled them into the South, where they could be sold for good money.

Even though the majority of Northerners did not want to associate with blacks, did not want them in their churches or working alongside them on their jobs, they were increasingly persuaded that black slavery as practiced in the South was an evil thing, even a sin against God. They heard abolitionist speakers say that slavery ought to "send a thrill of horror through the nerves of civilization. . . . So it might, if men had not found out a fearful alchemy by which [slavery] can be transformed into gold." A generation before, Northerners had not been so sure that slavery was an evil. But by the 1840s many believed it was; and some believed it passionately.

CHAPTER III

The Missouri Compromise Comes Apart

The rise of a new spirit in a society is a complicated thing. It is certainly true that a lot of Northerners who became abolitionists were driven by a feeling of hostility toward the South, as much as by concern for blacks. How widespread this feeling was in the North is difficult to know; but whatever the case, Southerners certainly felt that the abolition movement was basically an effort to hurt, or even destroy, the Southern society and bring the South under the command of the North. With such feelings afloat, compromise, after 1830, clearly was going to be difficult.

Not every American was caught up in the growing hostility between North and South. For one thing, there were many people on both sides who saw trouble ahead, and hoped to cool down passions before the crack widened. For another, a lot of people in the so-called western states, like Kentucky, Illinois, and Indiana did not feel they belonged to either side. Nonetheless, millions of Americans were intensely affected by the battle over slavery.

After the Missouri Compromise, for a moment things remained quiet.

There were now twelve slave states, twelve free ones, giving the South effective control, since southerners or men sympathetic to them sat in the presidency and it took two-thirds of each house to override a presidential veto. The balance was maintained in the Senate when, in 1836 and 1837, Arkansas and Michigan were admitted—one a slave state, one free.

But matters were marching to unhinge the Missouri Compromise. In the 1830s fervent abolitionists began petitioning Congress to write laws against slavery. These petitions were often very hostile to the South. In reaction, Southern congressmen managed to get through Congress a succession of "gag rules," which prevented Congress from considering, or even receiving, petitions against slavery. In 1844 Northern congressmen felt they had been pushed too far, and struck down the gag rules, but the effect had been to widen the divide between North and South.

Then came a cold wind from another direction. In 1821 Mexico achieved its independence from Spain after almost three hundred years as a colony. While it had an old and well-developed culture in what is now central Mexico, its outlying territories to the north were sparsely settled. This was a huge piece of land, including what is now Texas, New Mexico, Arizona, California, and portions of other states. In order to attract settlers, Mexico invited Americans into portions of Texas. Most of these new Mexican citizens were from the American South, and they brought with them hundreds of slaves. In 1836 the Texans fought their war of independence against Mexico. The Mexican slaughter of the brave—or foolish—little band defending the Alamo inspired Texan fighters, and finally they beat a larger Mexican army.

These Texans, we remember, were mainly American immigrants from the South. They expected to come into the United States as one or more states. However, President Andrew Jackson knew that the admission of Texas would once more raise the bitter controversy over slavery and divide the Democratic Party on the eve of an election. He stalled. His successor, Martin Van Buren also stalled, and so did William Henry Harrison and John Tyler.

But in 1844 James K. Polk was elected. Polk's election was taken by President Tyler to be a public endorsement of admitting Texas to statehood. He urged Congress to pass the necessary legislation, and in 1845 Texas was finally admitted as a slave state.

Polk had long eyed the vast, thinly settled western lands only loosely controlled by Mexico. In 1846 he contrived an excuse to go to war with Mexico. The fighting was bitter and cost 13,000 American lives, but the Americans won decisively. In the Treaty of Guadalupe Hidalgo of 1848, which ended the war, the United States got confirmation of its authority over Texas, as well as possession of California and the Southwest. These lands would sooner or later—and probably sooner—have to be cut up and admitted as states. The issue of slavery could no longer be avoided. (The story of the Texas, California, and Mexican War is told in more detail in the volume of the Drama of

President James K. Polk strongly favored the expansion of the United States into the west by whatever means. He pushed the nation into a war with Mexico that could have been avoided.

The acquisition of huge amounts of territory from Mexico as a result of the Mexican War opened up the possibility of several new states. This in turn raised the thorny question of whether such new states would be free or slave. Here, an artist's version of the landing of American troops at Vera Cruz, where the Americans won an important battle against the Mexicans.

American History called *Hispanic America, Texas, and the Mexican War* in this series.)

Americans were split several ways. There was, in 1848, a still-small minority of abolitionists in the North who would risk dividing the Union—even to the point of secession—to get away from slavery. Similarly, there was a small minority in the South who were willing to secede from the Union if necessary to preserve slavery. Others felt that the answer was to extend the Missouri Compromise and push the 36°30' line right across the country through California, with land to the south of it slave territory and land to the north free. Finally, there were those who felt it should be left to the citizens of the territories themselves whether or not they would permit slavery within their borders. The thinking of these people was that slavery was only profitable where you could grow crops like cotton. You could not grow cotton outside of the warm wet parts of the new territories, such as eastern Texas and southern California. As a practical matter, according to these people, slavery was not likely to exist in the more northern of the new states like Utah or Nebraska; why make a big fuss over a theory?

But even as passions were rising, something new sprung out of the ground that gave the controversy another twist. In 1848, some workmen constructing a mill on the huge Sutter ranch in California found gold in the mill stream. Although Sutter tried to keep the discovery quiet, word got out, and by 1849 tens of thousands of Americans were pouring into California. California became a whirl of rough mining camps, cities like San Francisco growing so fast that people lived in houses made of canvas tacked to frames—a place where fortunes were made in a morning and lost in an evening on the turn of a card. Very quickly California reached a population of 250,000, much more than the 60,000 people needed for statehood. The new Californians began vociferously demanding to become a state so that the national government could bring order to the rapidly growing, nearly lawless community. (The story of California and the gold rush is told in the volume *Hispanic America, Texas, and the Mexican War*.)

There was no avoiding a decision now. The debate in the U.S. Senate over freedom or slavery for California and the other new states produced some of the most stirring speeches ever made in that body. They showed the Congress, filled with men who passionately believed in differing principles, at one of its grandest moments. Three men who became heroes of that moment were Daniel Webster of Massachusetts, John C. Calhoun of South Carolina, and Henry Clay of Kentucky. All three were old and had fought many battles with and against each other in the Senate. All three had been unsuccessful contenders for the presidency. All three had taken stands on principle and had too many enemies to win the highest office.

Clay, aged seventy-three, was from a western state, and took it upon himself to work out a deal. The complicated Compromise of 1850, often also called the California Compromise, combined a number of points in

One of the greatest debates in the United States Congress came over the critically important issue of which new states would be slave or free. This debate pitted John C. Calhoun (left) of South Carolina and Daniel Webster (right) of Massachusetts against each other. Their speeches were widely printed in newspapers, and Webster's was memorized by schoolchildren for decades afterward.

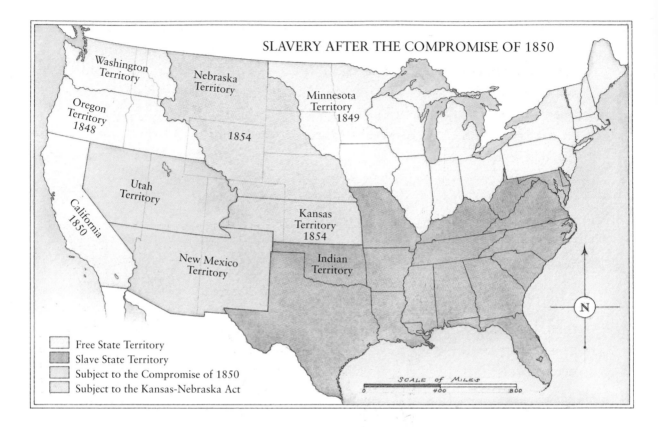

SLAVERY AFTER THE COMPROMISE OF 1850

Washington Territory

Oregon Territory 1848

Nebraska Territory

1854

Minnesota Territory 1849

California 1850

Utah Territory

Kansas Territory 1854

New Mexico Territory

Indian Territory

N

SCALE of MILES
0   400   800

Free State Territory
Slave State Territory
Subject to the Compromise of 1850
Subject to the Kansas-Nebraska Act

the dispute between North and South, trading off a little of this for a little of that. The main provisions were that California would come in as a free state, that was what the vast majority of the settlers there wanted. The rest of the land acquired from Mexico would be cut up into territories that could decide for themselves whether they would be free or slave. Since what they decided as territories was sure to be continued when they became states, the territorial constitutions became crucial. Everyone agreed, of course, that constitutionally the voters of every *state* could vote slavery up or down any time they wanted—and, indeed, as we have seen, by 1850 all the states north of Delaware had abolished slavery or watched it disappear.

In the Senate, Clay and Webster worked feverishly to push the compromise through. In one of the most famous speeches ever made in the Senate, Webster said, "I wish to speak today not as a Massachusetts man, not as a Northern man, but as an American . . . I speak today for the preservation of the Union. Hear me for my cause."

Calhoun, so sick and old that he could not deliver his speech himself, listened as it was read for him. The "cords of the Union" were breaking; the North must stop agitating against slavery if the Union were to be preserved. But neither the great speeches, nor Clay's constant bargaining, worked. There were too many on both sides who would not compromise. Finally Stephen A. Douglas, eventually to become famous in history for his debates with Abraham Lincoln, maneuvered the compromise through Congress one piece at a time. Only one out of five congressmen supported it as a whole; but there was enough support for each part of it to get them through one by one. The terms were that California would come in as a free state; the territories cut out of the New Mexico Territory would decide for themselves whether to permit slavery; the slave trade (but not slavery itself) would be abolished in Washington, D.C.; and there would be a strict new fugitive slave act.

Then during the months of 1851 and 1852 an antislavery newspaper, *National Era*, published in serial and then book form Harriet Beecher Stowe's novel *Uncle Tom's Cabin*. This book, written principally to demonstrate that good Christians could not be slaveholders, pictured so graphically and so emotionally the horrors of slavery that millions of white Americans, until now unconcerned about slaves, became convinced and committed abolitionists. The parting of the ways between North and South was approaching.

In history, unforeseen events have a way of upsetting apple carts. One such event was the discovery of gold in California, which drew a huge population into the territory. A second was the speed with which the land on the Great Plains west of the Mississippi was settled. Right along, the

Uncle Tom's Cabin written by Harriet Beecher Stowe, is one of the best known of American novels. It pictured the plight of slaves in the South very sympathetically, and helped to arouse opinion in the North in support of abolishing slavery.

compromisers had assumed that it would be decades before the issue of slavery would be raised again, and in the meantime perhaps the old wounds would have healed. But settlers poured westward, and suddenly there were tens of thousands of people out in lands almost unknown to whites ten years earlier, clamoring for statehood.

Thus, in 1854, only four years after the California Compromise had supposedly settled things, the statehood question was before Congress again, this time concerning what was called the Nebraska Territory. This huge area included the modern states of Kansas, Nebraska, and parts of North and South Dakota, Montana, Wyoming, Idaho, and Colorado. Much of it had been reserved for the Indians through treaties with the U.S. government, but in fact thousands of white settlers had moved in and started farming.

According to the Missouri Compromise of 1820, land in the Louisiana Territory north of the 36°30' dividing line, at the southern border of Missouri, would be free—except for Missouri itself. Northerners insisted that new states in Nebraska Territory must be free. But the California Compromise of 1850 had introduced the idea of "popular sovereignty" by which the people of new territories would decide about slavery for themselves.

The Nebraska problem was put before Congress by the formidable Senator Stephen Douglas, of Illinois, a fiery little man with big ambitions. Douglas proposed that the new territory be divided into two parts, called the Kansas Territory and the Nebraska Territory. The Missouri Compromise would be repealed and "popular sovereignty" would allow the residents of the territories to decide whether they would permit slavery or not. Douglas's bill would make it possible for lands above the old dividing line to become slave states.

Douglas's opinion was that the Nebraska Territories were not suitable for cotton-growing, so there would be no point in bringing slaves there. Why fight over an issue that as a practical matter didn't exist? Southerners in Congress voted for the Kansas-Nebraska Act, along with enough Northerners to pass it.

Some Southerners were unhappy with the Kansas-Nebraska Act. The Constitution allowed any American to move anywhere in the country he wanted, bringing his property with him. Slaves were property; and therefore, according to this way of thinking, slavery ought to be legal everywhere in the United States, even in places like Massachusetts, which had long since abolished it. This, however, was a minority opinion in the South. Most Southerners accepted the Kansas-Nebraska Act of 1854.

In the North it was another matter: millions of Northerners were simply outraged. To them, the Missouri Compromise was almost as sacred as the Constitution itself, and according to it, Kansas and Nebraska should be free. Clearly the two great sections of the American nation were on a collision course. One historian has said of the Kansas-Nebraska Act of 1854, "Probably no bill ever introduced to Congress was fraught with graver consequences."

Now that the status of the Nebraska Territory had been legally settled, people began to scramble for land there. Kansas, bordering on
Missouri, attracted a lot of immigrants from that state. Missouri was a
slave state. Many Northerners believed that if they did not act, immigrants from Missouri would fill Kansas with slaves, making it into a slave
state—whether there were actually any slaves there or not. At least they
would fill the territory with pro-slavery voters who would be there when
it came time to adopt a territorial constitution. A movement arose in the
North to encourage "free-soilers" to settle in Kansas to counteract the
pro-slave people. In fact, very few slaves were brought into Kansas, but
it was true that Missourians took up land claims there so they could vote
for a pro-slavery Constitution for Kansas. Tempers rose, a flash point
was reached, and open warfare broke out in Kansas between the free-
soilers and the supporters of slavery.

It is difficult today to know exactly who started the trouble. Both
sides seem to have been equally bloodthirsty. In November 1854, well
over a thousand "border ruffians" who favored slavery came into Kansas
from Missouri. In May 1856 some of them sacked the town of Lawrence.
In retaliation the abolitionist John Brown led a raid in Pottawatomie and
massacred some pro-slavery men. For four months a real war was fought
in which towns were pillaged and even burned, and people slaughtered.
Fighting died down by the fall of 1856, but about two hundred people
had been killed, and there were occasional outbursts and deaths almost
up to the Civil War.

With the passage of the Kansas-Nebraska Act and the fighting in
Kansas, a line was crossed. Attitudes in both North and South had hard-
ened. In Congress, which not long before had heard the generous, rea-
soned speeches of Webster and Clay, speakers openly insulted one another.
At one point Senator Charles Sumner of Massachusetts in an emotional
tirade viciously attacked the elderly Senator Andrew Butler of South
Carolina. Two days later Butler's young cousin, Preston Brooks, walked

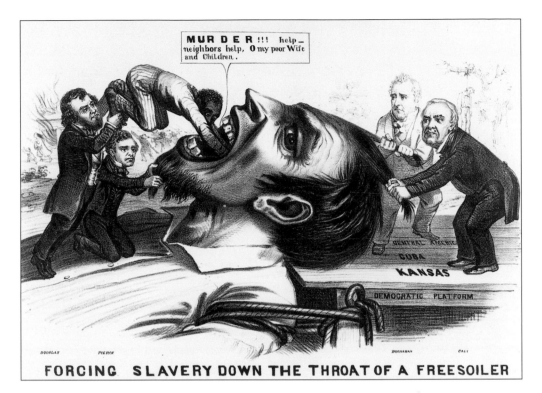

FORCING SLAVERY DOWN THE THROAT OF A FREESOILER

As tensions rose, some Southerners began claiming that the Constitution allowed slaveholders to bring their slaves into any state, free or slave. Northerners were outraged by the idea that they might have slaves among them. This cartoon shows (from left) Stephen Douglas, President Franklin Pierce, President James Buchanan, and Secretary of State Lewis Cass forcing a free-soiler to swallow slavery.

into the Senate and began beating Sumner over the head with a heavy cane, nearly killing him. None of the other senators came to Sumner's aid, and Brooks was later let off with a small fine. In the South, Brooks was praised as a hero, but in the North the attack was seen as a last straw. The spirit of compromise was dead.

American political parties, the Whigs and the Democrats, felt the effects immediately. Previously there had been Southerners and

Open warfare broke out in Kansas between free-soilers and advocates of slavery. This woodcut, made at the time, shows a gun battle between the two sides in a small Kansas town.

Northerners in both parties. But now Southerners, feeling that the Democratic Party was more sympathetic to their viewpoint, began to drift away from the Whig Party.

Meanwhile, in the North, a new party, called the Republicans, had been formed. At first it was only one among several new parties competing to replace Democrats and Whigs. In some states a party devoted to banning alcohol—the Prohibition Party—became strong; in others the anti-Catholic American Party, the so-called Know-Nothings, dedicated to restricting immigration, dominated. But finally, after the Nebraska Act and the Kansas War had so deeply divided Americans along north-south sectional lines, anti-Nebraska voters, a large share of Northern Whigs, Know-Nothings, and Free Soilers came together to support the new Republican Party. It was from the start a sectional party without any support in the South. The Party, however, did not favor abolition, and indeed many of its members were not only anti-black, but also anti-Catholic and anti-immigrant.

Thus, in the election of 1856 there were three major parties to vote for: the American Whigs, the Republicans, and the Democrats. There were also several smaller ones. The Democratic candidate, James Buchanan, won. The Republicans came in second. The Whigs, losing votes in the North to the Republicans and in the South to the Democrats, were a distant third. Now the United States had political parties aligned by sections of the country: the Democrats, still holding many northern members—the party of the South; the Republicans, with no southern members—the party of the North. The Whigs soon withered into insignificance.

The divide was deep, and it grew even deeper with one of the most notorious of all Supreme

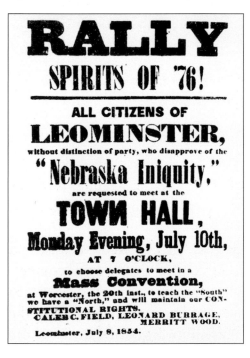

Debate over the Kansas-Nebraska question inflamed people on both sides. Here, a poster advertises a rally in Worcester, Massachusetts, against permitting slavery in the new western territories.

Joky Doy (seated) liberated a number of slaves in the western areas. He was captured and jailed, but his friends broke into the jail and freed him. Here they pose for a celebratory picture.

Court decisions, *Dred Scott* v. *Sanford*. Dred Scott was a slave who had been born in Virginia about 1803 and about thirty years later was taken to Missouri. Here he was sold to an army surgeon, who later took Scott to Illinois in 1833 and then to Minnesota, both free areas. When the surgeon died, his widow left Scott in Missouri, and went off to Massachusetts. Scott came under the legal control of her brother, John Sanford. In 1846 Scott was persuaded to sue for his freedom on the grounds that he had become free when he had lived in free territory. The case dragged its way through various courts until in 1856 it reached the

One of the most famous of all Supreme Court decisions came in the Dred Scott case. Chief Justice Taney ruled that blacks were not and could not be citizens. This ruling made many Northerners even more determined to risk war to end slavery.

U.S. Supreme Court. The Chief Justice at the moment was Roger Brooke Taney (pronounced Tawney), a slaveholder from Maryland. The majority of other justices were also Southerners. Taney's decision was long and complex, but it boiled down to a few points. For one, Taney insisted that not only slaves, but no blacks, free or slave, could be citizens. African Americans, he said, "had no rights which the white man was bound to respect." And he went on to say that Congress did not have authority under the Constitution to forbid slavery anywhere—nor could it authorize territories to forbid slavery within their borders.

This decision overturned the whole Missouri Compromise. Moreover, it ended the idea of popular sovereignty, under which territories could decide for themselves about slavery. This was the first time that the Supreme Court had declared a major Federal law unconstitutional. Historians today agree that Taney was not right: the Constitution did not forbid the Congress from making laws about slavery in the territories. One historian has written, "Behind his mask of judicial propriety, the Chief Justice had become privately a fierce southern sectionalist, seething with anger at "Northern insult and Northern aggression.'"

Southerners were jubilant about the Dred Scott ruling, but such celebration was simply waving a red flag in front of the North. It seemed to many that the Taney decision would force states like Massachusetts and Michigan to tolerate slavery in their midst if slaveholders chose to move there and bring their slaves with them. The Dred Scott decision made the chasm between North and South even wider and deeper.

It also caused serious problems for Stephen A. Douglas. One of the most celebrated politicians of the day. Douglas was expected to get the Democratic nomination for president, and might well win the upcoming 1860 election. But whatever position he took on the Dred Scott decision was bound to anger one side or the other. He chose the middle road. According to Douglas, Taney's decision was the law, like it or not. However, as a practical matter slaveholders were not likely to take their slaves into territories that were hostile to slavery, and the territory could in the end eliminate slavery merely by enacting no legislation to protect it. Under those conditions slaves could simply run away and no law would make that illegal. Southerners, of course, were outraged by this idea.

Douglas was ducking the issue, and there was one man in Douglas's home state of Illinois who was willing to stand up and say so. He was a tall, gangly, carelessly dressed lawyer who was born in Kentucky and reared on rough frontier farms. His name was Abraham Lincoln. (Readers interested in more detail about Lincoln can find it in the volume in this series called *The Civil War*.)

CHAPTER VI

An Important Man Enters the Scene

Abraham Lincoln's ancestors had originally come from Massachusetts and he shared the old New England ideas of self-improvement and following the moral path. Critically important for the history of the United States, Lincoln had, like many Americans, Norh and South, a reverence for the patriots who had gained America's freedom from the British, and an almost mystical belief in the importance of the Union they had forged.

Lincoln was not alone in this belief. We must remember that even as late as the 1850s, when Lincoln was emerging as a political figure, by far the majority of human beings lived in societies controlled lock, stock, and barrel by kings, queens, and chieftains and their small circle of aristocrats. Few people had anything like a vote at all; many, if not most, people lived as serfs and peons little different from slaves. Even in the more democratic nations, like England and France, a small handful ruled, and only a minority could vote.

The United States was not perfectly democratic: women could not vote or hold office, and of course neither could slaves or, indeed, except

Abraham Lincoln is undoubtedly our most celebrated president. The number of books about him runs into the thousands. The picture below shows Lincoln as he looked before he became president. This is from a print by the famous printmakers Currier & Ives, and hung in thousands of American homes.

The picture above shows Lincoln with a beard, as he looked when he was president.

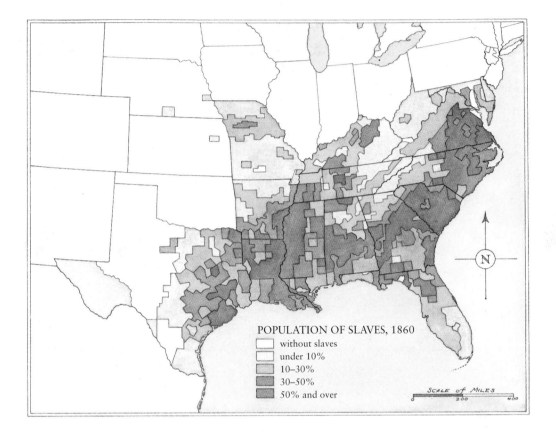

POPULATION OF SLAVES, 1860

☐ without slaves
☐ under 10%
▢ 10–30%
▢ 30–50%
▢ 50% and over

SCALE of MILES
0   200   400

in very rare instances, free blacks; nonetheless, it was certainly far ahead of the other major nations in democracy. To thoughtful people, a nation in which the citizens actually governed themselves, choosing their own leaders and having certain rights guaranteed them, was little short of a miracle. Such people believed that the United States must continue to set an example for the rest of the world, leading them toward democracy— as indeed it has done.

Thus, to a man like Lincoln, keeping the great American "experiment" going mattered not merely to Americans, but to the rest of humanity. And like other thoughtful people, Lincoln feared that if the nation split up, its democracy would be threatened. France was already attempting to take over Mexico. Powerful England wanted to get economic control of the Southern states, to guarantee a source of the cotton it needed for its textile factories. There was always the risk that a splintered nation would fall, a piece at a time, into the hands of foreign, or even homegrown, tyrants. Lincoln shuddered at this idea.

Along with his almost religious belief in American democracy, Abraham Lincoln was against slavery. In 1858 he told an audience that while he hated slavery, "I have always been quiet about it until this new era of the introduction of the Nebraska Bill began. I always believed that everybody was against it, and that it was in the course of ultimate extinction." Now he saw that people like Stephen Douglas did not much care about slavery either way. They just wanted to make sure that quarreling over it did not get in the way of other matters. Lincoln helped to start the new Republican Party in Illinois, which was against slavery. In 1858 the party named him to run for the Senate against Douglas.

The Lincoln-Douglas debates are among the most important of their kind in American history. Both men were eloquent speakers; both were willing to stand up for their beliefs. In opening his campaign, Lincoln gave a speech that one historian has said "signified a turning point in American political history." In that speech Lincoln said, "A house divided against itself cannot stand," and that "this government cannot endure permanently half slave and half free." It would have to be one or the other.

Lincoln was not an outright abolitionist, demanding the end of slavery. He certainly did not want to drive the South out of the Union, which would probably bring on war. He thought that if slavery were prohibited in new territories and was thus confined to the states of the old South, it would eventually die out of its own accord. But he believed that it ought to be the policy of the U.S. government to help that happen.

Stephen Douglas was a major figure in the United States of the time, a potential president. Perhaps the most significant thing he did in the

Stephen Douglas was expected by many to become president. His debates with Lincoln in the senatorial campaign in Illinois were widely reported all over the United States, and made Lincoln famous. Douglas won the election against Lincoln, but he would not take a strong stand against slavery; instead he looked for compromise, and was thus unpopular in the North. It was Lincoln who became president.

debates was to bring Lincoln before the American public and make him famous. Lincoln did not win Douglas's seat, although the vote was close, but by the end of the election he was seen as somebody who might become a presidential candidate himself.

However, events were outrunning the politicians. As the probable Democratic candidate in 1860, Douglas had the impossible task of straddling the widening chasm dividing North and South. By this time both sides were taking ever more extreme and rigid stands. In the South there was talk of bringing in slaves from Africa again, which had been forbidden for fifty years. Northerners were hardly going to allow this, and for the most part were adamant about letting new territories forbid slavery if they wished. Southerners, abiding by the Dred Scott decision, held that slavery should be allowed everywhere. This shows how aggressive Southerners had gotten: previously they had merely wanted to protect their right to keep slaves; now they were insisting on the right to open, not only northern territories, but also northern states, to slavery.

But there were hard-liners in the North, too. In October 1859 the violent abolitionist John Brown decided to incite a slave rebellion in Virginia. This was the same John Brown who had murdered pro-slavery men in Kansas, and had made raids into Missouri against slaveholders. He had much support in the North, and that October, with a tiny army of five blacks and sixteen whites, he made an attack on the government arsenal at Harpers Ferry in Virginia, just over the line from Pennsylvania. His idea was that local slaves would quickly join the fight, using arms captured from the arsenal. This would encourage slaves everywhere to revolt. At first the raid was successful:

John Brown as a young man, in a photograph showing the piercing eyes and determined mouth of a man who would stop at nothing to gain his ends.

Brown's men managed to cut the telegraph lines leading out of town and capture a rifle factory and the government arsenal. But the local militia and a company of U.S. Marines soon stormed Brown's position. Brown was wounded and his men killed or scattered. Brown was captured and soon condemned to be hanged. In one of his last letters he said that he may have lost his battle, but he would do greater good for his cause "by only hanging a few moments by the neck." It was certainly true. Brown was considered by some Northerners to be a fanatic, but others thought him a hero. He inspired the most famous of all Civil War songs, which

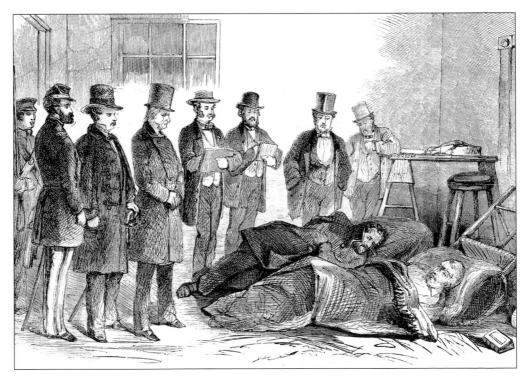

John Brown and a fellow conspirator, lying wounded after the raid on Harpers Ferry, where they are visited by the governor of Virginia, and some reporters and artists making sketches of the scene for newspapers. One of them made this sketch.

has the lines, "John Brown's body lies a-moldering in the grave, his soul is marching on."

Opinion in the South about John Brown was, needless to say, somewhat different. His raid on Harpers Ferry shocked Southerners. They now believed that there were people in the North—perhaps millions of them—who would risk death to take slavery away from them.

Significant numbers of leading politicians on both sides were no longer willing to compromise.

The first effects were felt by the Democratic Party at their national convention to nominate a presidential candidate in April 1860. Southern

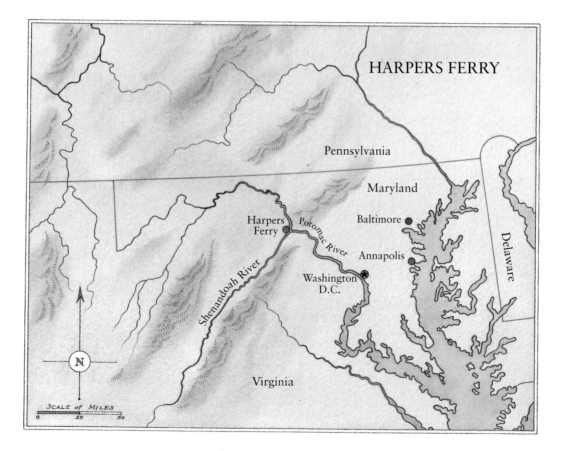

To many Northerners John Brown was a hero who had martyred himself for the cause of ending slavery. However, not all Northerners were opposed to slavery, and a great many of them who were opposed to slavery in principle did not really want to associate with blacks. These two cartoons, from the well-known magazine Vanity Fair, show antiblack sentiment. At left a giant black man is pictured as Samson tearing down the temple of the American Constitution. Below, some abolitionists with pinched faces dance a jig with a black woman who they have invited to join them.

delegates wanted the party to take a strong pro-slavery stand; northerners wanted otherwise. Eventually the Southerners abandoned the party and nominated their own candidate, John C. Breckinridge. The Northerners remaining in the party nominated Stephen Douglas. The Republicans nominated Lincoln. The national vote was strictly along sectional lines: Lincoln took the North, Breckinridge most of the South; Douglas and another Southern candidate took a few states apiece. Although Lincoln got only 40 percent of the total popular vote, he won enough states to give him a clear victory in the electoral college.

Although Abraham Lincoln personally hated slavery, he knew that he could not try to end it without driving the South out of the Union. He only wished to keep it from spreading into new places.

But that was enough for Southern politicians: in their view, the Constitution guaranteed all the right to their property wherever they moved it. You could not take somebody's hat away from him just because he moved from Georgia to New York: why, then, could you take his slaves from him? For years Southerners had talked about seceding from the Union if it looked like Northern politicians were going to get the upper hand. Finally, on December 20, 1860, South Carolina withdrew from the United States.

From the point of view of South Carolinians, they were only doing what the Revolutionaries of 1776 had done. They cited the principles of the Declaration of Independence that governments are established to protect the rights of the people, and if they don't protect, but violate them, then the people have a right—even an obligation—to withdraw from the government and establish a new one. According to the South Carolina "Declaration of Causes of Secession," the U.S. Constitution was a compact among equal sovereign states delegating certain limited powers to the central government. Since that government had exceeded its limits by failing to guarantee the rights of property (in slaves), states had a right to leave the Union and establish their own new governments. South Carolina withdrew from the United States by passing an "Ordinance to Dissolve the Union between the State of South Carolina and the other states . . ." that repealed the act of 1788 ratifying the Constitution and declared that "the Union now subsisting between South Carolina and other states under the name of the United States of America is hereby dissolved."

This engraving, made at the time, shows South Carolinians in their capital, Columbia, unfurling a "States' Rights" flag for the first time. The secession of South Carolina led other Southern states out of the Union.

The secession of South Carolina started a stampede. Over the next two months Mississippi, Florida, Alabama, Georgia, Louisiana, and Texas seceded and began to put together a union of their own. For the moment the states of the upper South, Virginia, Arkansas, Tennessee, and North Carolina, held back. (The slave states of Missouri, Kentucky, Delaware, and Maryland remained in the Union. So did the western part of Virginia, which broke off to become West Virginia.)

Historians today believe that Southern politicians in general overreacted to the election of Lincoln. As it would turn out, Lincoln would have gone a long way to conciliate the South, although whether he would have gone far enough to satisfy South Carolinians is an open question. At least it would have done southern politicians no harm to have waited. But many Southerners had grown impatient. Many did not believe that the North would fight to keep them in the Union; in any case, there was widespread feeling in the South that one proud, brave Southerner could easily whip a half-dozen Northerners.

When the South was beginning to form its own government, Lincoln was not yet president. According to the rule then, the new president did not take office until March. The president was still James Buchanan. The problem for Buchanan was this: the United States had all sorts of arms of government stretching out everywhere. There were, of course, government post offices all over the South in small towns and villages as well as cities. Port cities like New Orleans, Charleston, and Savannah had customs offices for collecting taxes on imports. There were army and navy bases, forts and encampments in the South as well. The southern states began taking over these forts and offices. In the case of customs offices and post offices, run by small staffs, that was not difficult; but it was not so easy to take over a well-armed fort or naval base.

One such strong point was Fort Sumter, situated on a small island in the harbor of Charleston. The South Carolina government demanded that the United States surrender the fort to it. South Carolina, after all,

James Buchanan, who was president when the Southern states started to secede, could find no plan of action, and did little while waiting for Lincoln to take over. Historians have speculated that Buchanan's "do nothing" posture might have at least delayed the outbreak of war.

was an independent country now, the rebels said, and could not allow a foreign nation to hold a fort in its waters. President Buchanan, terrified by the events rising up like a sea to engulf him, dithered: he would not give up Fort Sumter, but he would not do anything else, either. He tried negotiations, tried calming people down. But mostly he watched, and waited for his term to expire, when the hard decisions would fall on Lincoln's shoulders. South Carolina decided to starve out the troops at Fort Sumter under the command of Major Robert Anderson.

The American nation was in this situation, filled with apprehension and passion, when Abraham Lincoln was inaugurated as president in March 1861. His inaugural address was very conciliatory toward the South. While he said that he was duty bound to keep Federal control of the customs houses and army posts, he also said that he did not intend to

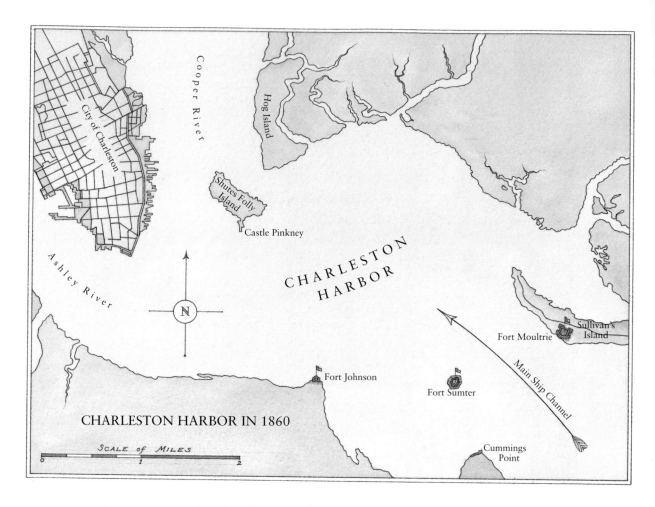

CHARLESTON HARBOR IN 1860

SCALE of MILES

send troops into the South. He asked Americans to slow down and consider; and he closed with these famous lines:

> We are not enemies, but friends. We must not be enemies. Though passion may have strained, it must not break, our bonds of affection. The mystic chords of memory, stretching from every battle-field [of the Revolution] and patriot grave to every living heart and hearth stone all over this broad land, will yet swell the chords of Union when again touched, as surely they will be, by the better angels of our nature.

But chords of Union did not touch the better angels of many people's natures. In April Lincoln decided to send food to Fort Sumter to keep it from being starved out. He told the South Carolina government that he would send only food and no weapons, if they would let the ship pass. On February 9 the seceding states had established the Confederacy, with Jefferson Davis as president. It was now up to Davis to decide what to do. He concluded, as the South Carolinians had concluded earlier, that as a sovereign nation, the Confederacy could not allow a foreign power to hold a strong point in its own waters. He ordered General Pierre Beauregard, the Southern commander at Charleston, to attack. Beauregard bombarded Sumter with five thousand shells, and within thirty-three hours the fort surrendered. This was open rebellion. Lincoln immediately called for 75,000 volunteers to put down the revolt, and four states of the Upper South that had held back—Virginia, Arkansas, Tennessee, and North Carolina—joined the Confederacy. A great, and tragic, war began.

The great question, of course, is this: was there any way the Civil War could have been avoided? Historians have been arguing this issue for over a century, and have never come to an agreement about it. Here, at least, are some of the points they have made.

For one thing, on both sides the extremists had an influence all out of proportion to their numbers. Fervent abolitionists were only a small minority in the North. A great many Northerners did not care one way or the other about slavery. Many others actually supported it, among them bankers and industrialists doing business with Southerners—a cloth manufacturer buying tons of cotton produced by slaves could hardly come out against slavery. Yet especially during the 1850s, abolitionists—Harriet Beecher Stowe, in particular—managed to convince many Northerners that slavery was evil, and that the South was therefore evil for permitting it.

Similarly, slavery was economically important to only a minority of

This blurry photograph shows a crowd of South Carolinians celebrating at Fort Sumter the day after it was surrendered by the Northern commander. With the fall of Sumter, the Civil War was on.

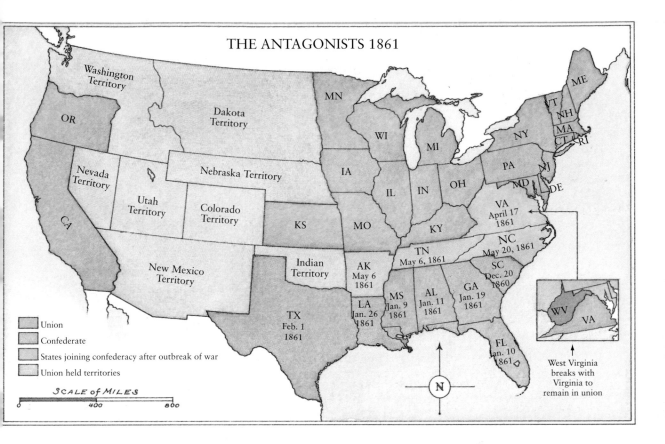

THE ANTAGONISTS 1861

Washington Territory

OR

Nevada Territory

CA

Utah Territory

Colorado Territory

New Mexico Territory

Dakota Territory

Nebraska Territory

KS

Indian Territory

TX
Feb. 1
1861

MN

WI

IA

MO

AK
May 6
1861

LA
Jan. 26
1861

MS
Jan. 9
1861

MI

IL   IN   OH

KY

TN
May 6, 1861

AL
Jan. 11
1861

GA
Jan. 19
1861

FL
Jan. 10
1861

ME

VT
NH
MA
CT RI

NY

PA
NJ

MD
DE

VA
April 17
1861

NC
May 20, 1861

SC
Dec. 20
1860

WV   VA

Union
Confederate
States joining confederacy after outbreak of war
Union held territories

SCALE of MILES
0   400   800

N

West Virginia
breaks with
Virginia to
remain in union

Southerners: as we have seen, about three-quarters of Southern families
did not own any slaves at all, and not more than 10 percent owned more
than a half-dozen or so. Yet by the 1850s supporters of slavery had
whipped up public opinion in the South to the point where nearly all
Southerners took it as a point of honor that they must not be deprived of
slavery by a dominating North.

Making matters worse, Southern extremists kept drawing the line further and further out. Originally all they had claimed was that slavery was
allowed under the Constitution, which was true. By the 1850s they were
insisting that the Constitution allowed them to bring their slaves anywhere in the United States—in effect claiming that no state could ban
slavery. This was a new interpretation of the Constitution, and one that
most historians today would not agree with.

But many Southern politicians were willing to take extreme stands like this because they believed they could always leave the Union if things didn't go their way. Indeed, at least a minority of Southerners thought they would be better off forming their own nation. Some abolitionists agreed: as one of them said, why not "let our erring sisters go"?

Yet these were minority opinions. At least one historian has calculated that outside of South Carolina, the majority of Southerners, even in deep South states like Louisiana and Mississippi, did not really want to secede, but were intimidated into voting for secession by the militant ones. Thus, on both sides white Americans were forced into taking sides on an issue that in an everyday practical sense did not mean much to many of them. But both sides had come to see slavery as an emotional *moral* issue. For North and South slavery came to be a point of honor: human beings do not easily give in on points of honor, and morality cannot be compromised.

Still, if people had known what they were in for—a four-year struggle costing about twenty billion dollars (about ten times the value of all the slaves in the United States in 1860), the destruction of the Southern economy and the lives of 620,000 young men—they might have been willing to give way on points of honor. Though Lincoln tried to calculate the costs, no one could foresee the wreckage the war would cause. Both sides believed they could win easily; both sides believed that the war would be over in a month, after a couple of battles. So they were willing to take up the challenge.

Beyond the slavery issue, there was the economic one. Southerners had more and more come to feel that they were falling under the thumb of the North. At the time the Constitution was written, it had seemed that the two great sections of the nation were about equally powerful; if anything, the South, led by Virginia with its brilliant politicians and thinkers like Washington, Madison, and Jefferson, seemed the more powerful. But the population of the North was increasing much faster than that of the South; the North had most of the nation's banks, and it had a large and growing industrial machine. Many Southerners were fearful of Northern dominance and wanted to fight back, some way, any way.

For these Southerners the Republican victory putting Lincoln in the presidency was the last straw. The Republicans were a *Northern* party, not a national one. Although the Republican Party did not promote abolition, it was openly anti-slavery. It opposed the extension of slavery anywhere with an eye to its ultimate elimination everywhere, even in the South. As a consequence, the party had not been able to campaign in Southern states. Republicans thus did not understand what Southerners were thinking as well as they might have. Further, they had not been forced to find ways to accommodate Southerners in order to get their votes. Similarly, Southerners, not knowing Republicans firsthand, pictured them as devils determined to destroy the Southern way of life. Ignorance of one people by the other prevented them from developing any sympathy for the other side.

Finally, there was the character of Abraham Lincoln. He was a sympathetic, sensitive man, but he was no pushover. If James Buchanan had gone on being president perhaps things would have turned out differently. Stalling for time, as Buchanan did, might have allowed tempers to cool off, and the hotheads to be pushed aside by more reasonable people. But that seems unlikely. Most historians believe that war would have come sooner or later anyway. But we cannot be sure.

However, it was Lincoln, and not Buchanan who was president as the crisis boiled to a head. He was, as we have seen, utterly committed to the preservation of the Union. For him there could be no compromising on that point. He would fight. Whether he would have done so if he could have foreseen the carnage the war would cause, we cannot know. But try as he might, no more could he count the costs than anyone else. And so he decided to hold Fort Sumter. And the war was on.

BIBLIOGRAPHY

For Teachers:

Current, Richard N. *Lincoln and the First Shot*. New York: J. B. Lippincott Co., 1963.

Elkins, Stanley M. *Slavery: A Problem in American Institutional and Intellectual Life. 3rd. ed.* Chicago: University of Chicago Press, (rev. ed.), 1976.

Fehrenbacher, Don E. *The Dred Scott Case: Its Significance in American Law and Politics*. New York: Oxford University Press, 1978.

Genovese, Eugene D. *Roll, Jordan, Roll: The World the Slaves Made*. New York: Pantheon Books, 1972.

Holt, Michael F. *The Political Crisis of the 1850s*. New York: John Wiley, 1978.

Jordan, Winthrop D. *White Over Black: American Attitudes Toward the Negro, 1550–1812*. Chapel Hill: University of North Carolina Press, 1968.

Mannix, Daniel, and Malcolm Cowley. *Black Cargoes: A History of the Atlantic Slave Trade, 1518–1865.* New York: Viking, 1962.

Stampp, Kenneth M., ed. *The Causes of the Civil War.* New York: Simon and Schuster, 1991.

Stegmaier, Mark J. *Texas, New Mexico, and the Compromise of 1850: Boundary Dispute and Sectional Crisis.* Kent, OH: Kent State University Press, 1996.

Thomas, Hugh. *The Slave Trade: The Story of the Atlantic Slave Trade, 1440–1870.* New York: Simon & Schuster, 1997.

Walters, Ronald G. *The Antislavery Appeal: American Abolitionism After 1830.* Baltimore, MD: Johns Hopkins University Press, 1976.

For Students:

Barrett, Tracy. *Harpers Ferry: The Story of John Brown's Raid.* Brookfield, CT: Millbrook Press, 1993.

Herda, D. J. *The Dred Scott Case: Slavery and Citizenship.* Springfield, NJ: Enslow Publishers, 1994.

Katz, William Loren. *Breaking the Chains: African-American Slave Resistance.* New York: Atheneum Publishers, 1990.

Lester, Julius. *To Be a Slave.* New York: Dial, 1968.

McKissack, Patricia C., and Frederick McKissack. *Rebels Against Slavery.* New York: Scholastic, 1996.

Meltzer, Milton. *All Times, All Peoples: A World History of Slavery.* New York: Harper & Row, 1980.

Ofusu-Appiah, L. H. *People in Bondage: African Slavery in the Modern Era.* Minneapolis: Runestone Press, 1993.

Stepto, Michele, ed. *Our Songs, Our Toil: The Story of American Slavery as Told by Slaves.* Brookfield, CT: Millbrook Press, 1994.

INDEX

JAMES LINCOLN COLLIER is the author of a number of books both for adults and for young people, including the social history *The Rise of Selfishness in America*. He is also noted for his biographies and historical studies in the field of jazz. Together with his brother, Christopher Collier, he has written a series of award-winning historical novels for children widely used in schools, including the Newbery Honor classic, *My Brother Sam Is Dead*. A graduate of Hamilton College, he lives with his wife in New York City.

CHRISTOPHER COLLIER grew up in Fairfield County, Connecticut and attended public schools there. He graduated from Clark University in Worcester, Massachusetts and earned M.A. and Ph.D. degrees at Columbia University in New York City. After service in the Army and teaching in secondary schools for several years, Mr. Collier began teaching college in 1961. He is now Professor of History at the University of Connecticut and Connecticut State Historian. Mr. Collier has published many scholarly and popular books and articles about Connecticut and American history. With his brother, James, he is the author of nine historical novels for young adults, the best known of which is *My Brother Sam Is Dead*. He lives with his wife Bonnie, a librarian, in Orange, Connecticut.